*From
the
Balcony*

From the Balcony

Poems
by
Marcus Reichert

Introduction by Antony Copley

Paintings by Marcus Reichert

ZIGGURAT BOOKS
International

From the Balcony: Poems by Marcus Reichert
Copyright © 2013 by Marcus Reichert
Illustrations Copyright © 2013 by Marcus Reichert

All rights reserved. Except for brief passages quoted in a newspaper, magazine, radio, or television program, no part of this book may be reproduced in any form or by any means, electronic or mechanical, including photocopying and recording, or by any information storage and retrieval system, without permission in writing from the Publisher.

Front cover painting:
Balcony Window 1989 by Marcus Reichert

UK office: 27 St. Quentin House, Fitzhugh Grove,
London SW18 3SE, England
Editorial office: 6 rue Argenterie,
30170 St. Hippolyte du Fort, France
Enquiries: zigguratbooks@orange.fr

Printed by Imprint Digital, Upton Pyne, Exeter

Distributed by Central Books Ltd.
99 Wallis Road, London E9 5LN, England
Tel UK: 0845 458 9911
Fax UK: 0845 459 9912
Tel International: +44 20 8525 8800
Fax International: +44 20 8525 8879
E-mail: orders@centralbooks.com

First Edition

ISBN 978–0–9573911–1–6

Other Ziggurat Books by
Marcus Reichert

Percy Lifar: A Tragicomedy
Lost Lake: Early Poems
Confessions: Poems
Hoboken: A Novel
Art & Ego: Marcus Reichert
in Conversation with Edward Rozzo
Displaced Person:
Poetry, Pornography and Politics
(Selected Writings 1970–2005)

Marcus Reichert, St. Hippolyte du Fort, 2012 (Hugh Stewart)

Acknowledgements

Thank you to Henry Ralph Carse for his encouragement, to Antony Copley for his introduction, and to my life-long editor Sally MacLeod.

M.R.

Marcus Reichert is a poet and a painter who has also worked in film. His film works are held in the Archive of the Museum of Modern Art, New York. His Crucifixion paintings have been described by Richard Harries, the Bishop of Oxford, as being among the most disturbing painted in the 20th Century. Marcus Reichert lives and works in the south of France.

Antony Copley is an Honorary Senior Research Fellow and Honorary Reader in the School of History, University of Kent. He is Academic Adviser to the Gandhi Foundation (UK), and a Fellow of the Royal Historical Society and a Fellow of the Royal Asiatic Society. He is a regular reviewer for the Journal of the Royal Asiatic Society and has published books on sexual morality in France, evangelical missionaries in India, and the Indian politicians, Gandhi and Rajagopalachari. His *Music and the Spiritual: Composers and Politics in the 20th Century* is published by Ziggurat Books International.

From the Balcony

The poetic work is sacred in that it is the creation of a topical event, 'communication' experienced as *nakedness*. It is self-violation, baring, communication to others of a reason for living, and this reason for living 'shifts.'

Colette Peignot aka Laure, 1903–1938

Knowing must therefore be accompanied by an equal capacity to forget knowing. Non-knowing is not a form of ignorance but a difficult transcendence of knowledge. This is the price that must be paid for an oeuvre to be, at all times, a sort of pure beginning, which makes its creation an exercise in freedom.

Jean Lescure on the painting of Charles Lapicque, 1956

Contents

Introduction xvii
A Common Humanity
by Antony Copley

I.

Indelibly Marked 3

Lips and Leaves 4

As You Lie Within 5

All Things Unknown 7

Corridor of Light 8

Now Linger in Shadow 9

Her Crown of Thorns 10

She Said 12

She Walks On 13

Orchid 14

The Long White Vessel 15

Our Pale Hands 17

Nobody Is Just Nothing 18

A Voice Is Heard 20

And the Sea Drifted 21

Rivers 23

Fragment 24

Slanting Limb 25

As the Wind 26

The Time It Takes 27

The Bowl 28

The Drops of Rain 30

The Love That Lingers On 31

II.

Volga 37

Rome 38

The Life of the Mind 40

Garden of the Unborn 42

The Opulent Rose 46

We Become 47

Drawing a Robin 48

Stray Leaf 49

Mr. & Mrs. Blackett 51

There Stands the Enemy 55

Psychotic Poem 57

Who Could Be Ruder 58

Her Food Being Hot 59

Diary 60

The Upper Room 61

The Frog and the Flower 65

The Roses 66

Little Birds 67

The Wind 68

After the Fourth 69

The Foaming Crease 72

Introduction

A Common Humanity
by Antony Copley

Hegel ranked prose over poetry. It achieved a higher expression of consciousness. If one might disagree with his ranking, the interpretation feels valid. Poetry always seems to hover just beyond consciousness, suggestive rather than explicit. The poetry of this new collection falls into the suggestive in Part One, more explicit in Part Two. But the poetic language is always accessible, free of conceit and affectation, pleasingly clear and honest. Here is poetry that needs no introduction. The poems speak for themselves.
The poems of the first half are poems of mature love. Some are elusive and need some teasing out. There are several long narrative poems in the second half, evoking those wonderful narrative poems of C P Cavafy and drawing one into the enigmatic film world of Jean Cocteau, Jean Marais walking through those strange haunted country palaces.

In Part One we start with poems on the consolations of physical love. *As You Lie Within* promises such consolation after illness. I take *All Things Unknown* to be reflections on being *awoken* by a child crying. Very ordinary situations inspire the poems, reflecting on comings and goings at a railway station in *Corridor of Light*, swimming out to sea in *Now Linger in Shadow*. There can be sharp exchanges between the lovers, he acknowledging his 'infernal lying' in *She Said*. Do we deceive ourselves as to our true identities:

This idea, he thought, we have of ourselves
is something quite different from what we are
(*Orchid*)

With *The Long White Vessel* we have an early taste of a longer narrative poem on lovers on board whilst the crew are ashore.

And what is happening in *Nobody Is Just Nothing*? Rueful reflections on the hatred of the male for the female, worse, to hide from the truth than face it? Then in *A Voice is Heard* comes the message of this collection:

If there is a life unloved
let it be at least not a selfish life
let it be a life of sacrifice
guided by this unknown love
for tender leaves do bind us to
ourselves, one to another.

This is a message of a common humanity. There is a wonderful expression of triumph of love over adversity in *And the Sea Drifted*:

the hammer that fashions
our hopes into a million
unbearable little things

Part Two begins with *Volga*, a poem dedicated to Andrei Tarkovsky. *The Life of the Mind* has a kinship with an earlier poem – trains coming and going – its theme the transience of life. Then comes the first of the longer narrative poems *Garden of the Unborn*, morbid thoughts on the death of the father, on the mother's rejuvenation with his death, together with 'that sorry boy', the narrator, brooding on the sadness of his parent's marriage. Could he admit to the pain of this history? But it is a reflection of humanity in the poetry that he imagines his parents subsequently happily reconciled in death.

And we have a truly frightening poem of a desiccated marriage, echoing that famous sculpture by Keinholz, *this interminable union*. Little redemptive humanity here, it has to be said. Then comes the first of poems from the depths, a poem about a child murderer – in fact a soldier on a deluded spiritual mission –

There Stands the Enemy, and something truly extreme, a poem about the murderous feelings of an abused child, now an adult, for his mother, *Psychotic Poem*. The poem *Who Could be Ruder*, about the resentment of the elderly for those still fit and well, reminded me of that bitter memoir *Bad Blood* by Lorna Sage.

What is going on in another of those Cavafyesque poems *The Upper Room*? Is this another poem about a failure to understand the father? In fact it is a poem about a lonely man seeking comfort in a brothel, the ambiguous figure in the wheelchair its 'madam.'

After the Fourth is the last of the long poems narrated by a family friend both remembering a storm on the Aegean and the couple's seven-year-old child experiencing a similar storm at his home in America. The one poem that defeated me was *The Foaming Crease*. Is it saying we alone can answer for our actions? In fact the poem relates to an arson attack on a café, the townspeople coming out in the middle of the night to witness the building burning.

With regard to the two epigraphs the poet has chosen to begin this collection, do the poems live up to Colette Peignot's belief that poetry should express 'self-violation, baring, communication to others of a reason for living?' Indeed, there is a rawness here, both inherent in any expression of physical intimacy and in the way we see our parents. For a sense of 'shift,' however, and this is to be pedestrian, this could only be demonstrated if the poems were in chronological order, but a reason for living is presented here, in that underlying common humanity of the text.

There are two ways to respond to Jean Lescure's almost impossible aspiration for painting, doubtful and hopeful. Can we in fact abandon or transcend consciousness? Is this dream of a completely fresh beginning feasible, even desirable? Only the most radical rejection of the material world could facilitate such a fresh start. On the other hand, maybe it is not quite so complicated: can we not give expression to emotions direct from the subconscious, bypassing conditioned reflexes, and so tap into the spiritual?

I.

Indelibly Marked

Indelibly marked, the love
of one stranger to the next,
this unintelligible moment
shared without longing:
at the bottom of the sea
our embracing fires endure.

In the tongue that touches
no words, in the eyes that
see only enfolding darkness,
in the ears that hear only
a voice articulating heat,
stirs the centre of the rose.

Lips and Leaves

Her face so round,
her lips the leaves
that flutter down
to lift and ease
the surrendering sounds
of nights that bleed
one into the next;
until next
he receives
her awakening pleas,
but gentler now
comes the sound
of his reprieve
as they come down –
those lips,
those leaves,
to lift and ease.

As You Lie Within

As you lie within
the wake of a tide
of indifference,
remember always
that that same tide
will lead you to me.

As you lie within
the sombre waters
of yet another drowning,
remember that the
breath that will bring
you back to life is mine.

As you lie within
the cold confines
of your hospital bed,
remember that
the awakening of
your pulsing heart
is the passion
I give wanting you.

As you lie within
the floating world of
many, many tomorrows,
remember that each
of them was, for me,
mine to live with you.

As you lie within
the smouldering sweat
of your final undoing,
remember that
the heart of all pain
is the self-same heart
of all joy and true.

All Things Unknown

All things unknown, these
quiet hours insist we respect
the travails of the child,
our unsudden awakening
resplendently innocent,
crowned with conviction.

Kindness scattered round us,
our shadows precede us,
but we need not glance back
as the past doggedly nudges
us on to our sovereign liberation
beyond the earth's dominion.

Ahead, another awaits us,
a friend that is *like-flesh*,
a spirit to enfold and
to be warmly enfolded.
How shall we know him?
we ask, already knowing.

Our companion keeps no secrets,
he confides in us, his worries ours,
and we determine to go on, albeit
indeterminably; breaking sticks
grinding out their music in the sun,
they too wonder at our movements.

Corridor of Light

Threatening corridor of light
ringed by daffodils
drags me along to an uncertain fate.
The air that sparkles
on my tongue is the same air
that millions before me tasted
as their sinking ship went down.
The unfurling of the flag
of no nation, only conviction,
led me to this place that moves
along upended, like a cyclical wind.

What time is his train to arrive,
what time is hers to depart?
How many disruptions lie waiting
between here and there,
between nobody and nothing?

The dove lands on my window sill
and looks to see who is looking back.
But it is only me and my beating heart,
it is only me escaping into another me
who lives a great distance from this world.

Now Linger in Shadow

Shield my eyes from this light
and build a wall around me
so that I can let my desolation
drift away into the trees, into
the flowers, into the sky that
reaches down to caress
the tumbling vines. Our hearts
beat solemnly with the beauty
of this imperfect day, our first
quiet moments spent breathing
together, not alone, not lost.
Let us only now linger in shadow,
imagining that day when we will
swim together out to sea from
this very spot where we first
studied each other's faces.

Her Crown of Thorns

Her crown of thorns
fell away as the heat
of day rose to bless
the demurring flowers;
their silken heads,
that morning bathed in dew,
now welcomed the breeze's
slow majestic sighing,
and the light that glimmered
in her eyes from without
was not the emptiness within
as in harmony with
the sultry rhythm of the day
her heart began to sing.

When you're as old as I
you'll understand why,
she heard her lover say.
But he wasn't really
any older than she
and she knew this
and he knew it too.
But they both took comfort
in one knowing that
the other knew and
so nothing would ever change,
nothing would ever
come to fall between them
as do the leaves
between the trees.

Her crown of thorns
fell away as in the evening
she stood as if between
the pages of another day
lost in contemplation,
its hours having shifted
as had the sultry heat,
its interminable rise and fall
now blessedly complete.

And evening found itself
there about her
and sighed the sighs
of the day's idling departure,
as the breezes that had come
in the heat of the day
crept away over the tender grasses
that in their quiet way
now contentedly held her gaze.

She Said

Feet made of clay, he said.
Nay, she said.

Head made of bread, he said.
Dead, she said.

The apple fell
into the well
and made a sound
like sighing.

The bell it rang
and the angels sang
as if the clouds
were crying.

The heavenly hill
rises still,
the little lambs
nestled in a row,
their purity
somehow implying

that what she'd said,
without having
to think too much,
was truer still
in its simplicity
than his infernal lying.

She Walks On

She walks on,
proud and true,
like a flower
riding a pliant lapel.

Orchid

As ordinary, he knew, as an orchid,
and so he was afraid to touch her,
lest she fly away, or, more likely, melt.

This idea, he thought, we have of ourselves
as something quite different than what we are,
what use is it to anyone but a psychologist?

The rain clamoured harder on the dome
of the umbrella whose shaft he held
between them like an arrow waiting
to be harnessed to the wind and then
set sailing on its way to meet the sun.

The Long White Vessel

1.

The long white vessel drifts
on the evening water below
the villa on its burnt hill.
He lurches up out of the sea,
climbing the chrome ladder
to find her on a chaise piled high
with organdy pillows, her bikini
golden, her pampered flesh
gleaming darkly with uneasy luck.

Pale and naked, he kneels before her,
slack in the obsolete light of her eyes.
His gaze is grim, his determination
Promethean, while hers sparkles harder.
No need for taunting in her smile,
no need for sassy belligerence.
Their slippery figures, now entangled,
writhe disjointedly and duskily drink,
for the reptilian hour of lust is struck.

2.

He balances precariously on the stern,
his toes, like talons, gripping the edge.
He has bathed and dressed in white,
while she, sitting sipping her drink, has
thrown on a robe, shrouding her bosom.
What solace is this sea, as if it were
about to suck them down in its maw?
A sideways glance and the yacht's crew
can be seen shortening the distance,
returning from the old harbour town,

muscles limp with laughter, in their skiff.
Lights glimmer dimly in the villa's windows
and its shadow, in the retiring moonlight,
allows its long carpet to the water's edge.

He goes to her, she reaches for his hand,
and he draws the tides into his taut belly
as she searches his face, finding no mirror.
Now she rises and eases her way below,
where her confidence resides unconcerned,
not wanting to know the sullen pulsations
of every last winter spent waking alone.
Out on the water no murmuring regret,
only the rocking of oars hoisted aloft.
He welcomes the men home to their sea,
knowing they care little for mute tragedy.

Our Pale Hands

You'd dressed for the occasion,
put on make-up, blithe aplomb.
What age were you then, hiding
within the grove of ripening fruit
trees that brush aside glimpses
of consternation, confusion, and
the awkwardness of pleasure?
Childlike rhythm of your feet
that haunt the tiles with your
approach, not so unsure, not so
invulnerable to the sensations
that would join our pale hands.

Nobody Is Just Nothing

She called down from a window
high above the sunken street:
"Nobody is just nothing,
so worthless and afraid —
everything he says to me
is filled with his hatred!"

There was a clock on the building
that faced the fountain, but neither
ran backwards like the thoughts
that ran in my head searching
for a reason to not run in circles.

My white sleeve stood out
in the raw evening light like
the wounded branch of a tree —
there was flesh within this flesh,
there were green veins and red.

Now what if I lifted my hand
to signal the end of something
unheard of, something unknown?
What if not knowing was worse
than knowing everything at once?

How many songs had I sung and
forgotten for no reason whatsoever,
how many nights had I stood
on that stage and sung my heart out,
singing my heart into forgetting?

Where has she gone now that
the window is empty, but for
the words that will echo forever,
never escaping this town or
the trees of the darkening forest?

A Voice Is Heard

There is a wisdom in the world
that is living, and this is what
we must accept, but accept not
misshapen assurances dealt by
a chaotic hand in the dizzying
light of so many unholy days.

If there is a life lived unloved,
let it at least not be a selfish life.
Let it be a life of sacrifice
guided by this unknown love,
for tender leaves do bind us to
ourselves, one to another.

And the Sea Drifted

And the sea drifted
around her feet
like angels circling
to take her home.

Her dignity would remain
resolute, unbroken by
the hammer that fashions
our hopes into a million
unbearable little things.

The tidy gathering
of morning breezes
would rise again
with the same joy
that held each day.

But what waited in the midst
of our longing for her hours
to never end, to never cease
holding us inside, to always
tenderly be both hers and ours?

There was nothing
anyone could do
but love her still,
for she was someone
who loved in return.

Let her voice sing into us,
let her hands feel ours
gathering her up,
our souls circling
round her.

Let her joy be hers
and ours to hold,
as we hold her
at the very edge
of this nonsensical sea.

Rivers

Rivers of fire, rivers of blood
are drowned in
the heaping sands of forgetting.

When I was twelve I wrote:
Younger among valleys of lead,
the remaining become the dead.

As I hide my face
against the tree
that is Jesus' thigh,
so I hide my face
against the shame of life.

Fragment

Warmth, comfort, food,
the waters of healing,
the touch that shares in
our suffering and releases
us from our isolation for
brief moments eternal.

Slanting Limb

Slanting limb calling to
winged shapes so high,
please identify us now,
ourselves unknown.

Look to our joy,
you there beckoning,
look to our love
there in the light.

As the Wind

As the wind
enfolds the dove,
confounding time,
denying place,
I hold your love
inside me.

The Time It Takes

The time it takes,
despicable purgatory,
in a friend's dying.,
I am broken,
I am rude.

Is it you or me
who is dying?
What feelings
do we have
for ourselves,
if living
is not dying?

His body dead on the street,
a body alive in her womb,
let us sing without trying.

The Bowl

He found her bereft,
squeezing her milk
into her dead baby's bowl,
and knew he must
take her home to sleep.

The bats came out
as usual that evening
but this evening
they found the flies
swarming over
the bowl of milk,
and fed for a moment
in swooping delight.

When at last she spoke,
she said she needed
even more to love than give,
but the curtain of light
that surrounded her
kept her from these things.

The bats came to
cover her that night,
black blanket quivering,
and she knew she must
accept the light,
serene in her isolation,
while humanity would
have itself for itself,
to be cherished forever
for itself, and of itself,
even after the fall.

The curtain of light
would lift and take her
through the night,
while the baby's bowl
would keep her
from the plight
of friend and foe.

The Drops of Rain

The drops of rain
that fall
from her mouth
into mine
are warmer than
the rocks
that cradle
the sleeping snakes
who bathe
in the noonday sun.

The Love That Lingers On

1.

The love that lingers on
is not an unbridled love,
not a chaste love, but
a love of an unknown
magnitude. Neither is it
a love of convenience,
nor virtue, nor believing.
It is a mysterious love
commanding the currents
deep in the soul, slowly
emptying that perilous mine
of its unyielding diamonds;
there glimmer the dark faces
of the men who die reaching
for a light they can hold,
to carry with them back
into the depths of unloving,
a light to sweep the misery
from the path of their labours,
a yearning light beyond
reason, or merely wanting.

2.

Had he forgotten
how to love?
It wasn't a matter
of how, but with
each hour of each
day she had come
to wind herself
about him. And

the deeper he went
into the darkness
the more her light shone
to light his way back.

II.

Volga

Its deep roaming currents
reaching under us
to loft us heavenward,
the vast river embraces us.
Its arms are the arms
of the willowy serpent
who breathes life into
the brains of dreaming men
who want nothing more
than the pungent scent
of the river forever ebbing
inward from flesh to vein,
to bone, to selfless thought.

Angels are singing in the light
that this river each day
consumes to nourish the night,
its one and only love.

for Andrei Tarkovsky

Rome

The cars that stopped
and started
have stopped,
as has the heart of the city.

The solitary tiger
on his ledge
no longer looks down
stoically upon
the thronging masses,
but gazes inward
at another world.

He recalls his capture
at the edge of
the River Styx,
having quietly endured
unending captivity.

No one of merit
is left to admire him
in his subjugation,
only vagrants stalking
much lesser prey.

Once there was Mussolini,
his opera an epitome
of vainglorious enchantment,
once there was Nero,
his succulence matched only
by the thirst of his companions,
once there was the young Dante,
doubt his sole preoccupation.

The fires that descended
the stairs of these buildings,
the tiger knows,
were the wrathful waters
of an exalted god's
perverse inundation,
creeping stains that still glow
on the map of the night,
like a million gleaming eyes.

The tiger wondered,
feeling the net once again
hugging his ribs,
if being turned to stone
was perhaps a better fate
than suffering the deprivations
of other fleshbound beings.

It was a sad state of affairs,
what had happened to Rome,
the tiger concluded,
but somehow knew
it had happened before.

The Life of the Mind

Where does the life
of the mind go
when the Number 9 Bus
passes you by
leaving an indistinct trail
of something like smog
for a block or two,
shifting the leaves
and tormenting the bees
whether the season be
summer or fall?

And where have all
the winters flown
for that matter,
the ones with
the Christmas clowns
driving their cars
through the ruins
of lost civilizations
like plastic toys
scattered over
the living-room carpet?

And further to that,
what of the springs
that sent young hearts sailing
into the great unknown
of another unthinking embrace?

Yes, all of that knowledge
it was all so immediate,
as if the life of the body
had a mind of its own.

But what do you
really think now that
the Number 9 Bus
has gone
and you've been
left wondering
where you were going,
or going to go,
and where
it might take you –
your solitary mission –
surely not
to the end of your day.

Garden of the Unborn

VIEWING

1.

The room was blue, the same vapid blue
as the sky beyond the window with its
synthetic orange drapes. I looked around
at the grey metal chairs, the marble squares
of the linoleum floor, at my mother.

The synthetic orange drapes
were hanging inside his skull,
the grey metal chairs his bones,
the marble squares of the linoleum floor
his teeth locked together behind his lips,
no joy to empty out with his breath.

He's dead, isn't he? I said to myself.
Somehow he looked truer to himself,
his face a pale landscape of memories,
none vital enough to reach up and
touch me. Unable to love in life,
unwilling to realise in death what
 anyone might need from him now.

The stupid suit, where did he get it?
And the bland tie? I gave that to him.
And what about the big manly rings?
They must mean something to someone.
His face, as always, so solemn, so stern,
so empty of anything resembling the truth.
And the pancake make-up – look at it,
he's become the thing he always feared:
himself, vessel of ephemeral beauty,

sex-object to be randomly desired and,
igniting pride, confoundingly indulged.

2.

I like this room, the same vapid blue
as the sky outside. The grey metal chairs
and the linoleum floor with its marble squares.
The synthetic orange drapes now shimmering
like plaits of hair beyond the open coffin.
The suit, the tie, the big masculine rings.
Those big masculine rings signify something,
although I don't recall how special they are.
His handsome face as always so solemn,
but no longer quite so inscrutably stern,
the pancake make-up making him pink
and nearly perfect, someone to admire.

'Looks like himself,' murmured my mother
and, bringing on the pain, reached for my hand.

Even my father's death
was secure in its logic –
unable to love in life,
unwilling to realise in death
what anyone might need
from him now.

And there she was beside me,
eyes brimming with tears,
my mother, so very alive.
She was bursting with life,
now that he was dead.

'Hello Anthony,' I heard someone say,
'how are you and your mother doing?'

BURIAL

The enormous live oaks held the sky at bay,
only the tiniest puddles of sunlight sparkling
here and there over the dark warm ground.
It was thought to be a privilege to lie amongst
the righteous here interred and my father
had worked hard to join them. He had succeeded
in business, he had contributed to the community,
he had gone to the right church. He had proven
his worth, while living as selfishly as possible.

Everyone assembled by the grave I knew,
even the children of children who
had watched over me when I was a child,
and everyone, in whatever small way they could,
helped those of us who might momentarily
lose our way to find our way back to the source,
back to the all-embracing world of God's love.
It had been Lucy who had first breathed God's love
into Leonard's sad life. She had baked his bread,
she had made his bed, she had borne his only
legitimate child, and that sorry boy was me.

There she stood in the soothing shade,
her flesh plushy, as pampered as ever,
her toes pointed girlishly inward
as if forming the bow of a glorious little boat
that would, with the Lord's help, find its own way
to heaven's shore. There, at last, she and Leonard
would be at peace together. There, at last,
they would find happiness in each other's arms.

This was my prayer for them, there under the trees,
within that moment, a secret unselfish prayer.

HEREAFTER

I parked in their driveway,
the sky gone as grey as their house,
looked at nothing and began to cry.
But I was looking at something,
my hands, the steering-wheel.
I was looking at myself
and what I saw was terrible.
This must be corrected, I knew,
as the tears tasted salty and sweet.
I would never be weak again,
I would never allow another
to contemplate me as I was now
in my weakness, in my shame.
I would be smarter than my real self,
to be left in the dust of this day,
and only I would know what
I had been for so many years.

One day I might reveal this
to a woman, a woman very close
to my real self, to the weaker self
I had once been and today discarded.
But before I would allow that ever
to happen, I would make her like me.
I said a prayer for her then,
there in their driveway,
within that moment of resolve,
a very special secret prayer.

The Opulent Rose

The images
have become
too abundant
for the multitude
of humanity
to harvest.

However we find
such clarity
in the opulent rose
that we regain
our footing.

We are not undone
by diversity
but refreshed
by the certitude
of living sensation.

When memory
becomes a burden,
and speculation
an impediment,
the opulent rose
burns brightly.

We Become

Jorge Luis Borges said,
in so many words,
that when we read a book
we become the author.
This is an unappreciably
bold statement.
I know what he means
but I resist the idea.
Would Borges also say
that when we look
at a painting
we become the painter?
We like to think
that the traces
of our own particular existence
that are in our work
are ours alone, even if
we are digging a ditch.
Is everyone then
everyone else,
are the marks we commit
to any surface
there to be transmuted
by the participant
into a universal *us*?
Perhaps for Borges
the visceral world
was also the world
of the mind and this
I can accept.

Drawing a Robin

There's a robin outside the window.
Is that what a robin looks like?
How do I make a robin?
I'll start with the robin's eye.
The robin's eye looks a little like
the girl's eye in the movie last night,
when the girl turned her head
to look up at the moonlit clouds,
just before she leapt into the sea
from the shifting deck of the ship.
Yes, this is the robin's eye.
Now for the rest of the robin,
but the robin is gone. What did
the rest of the robin look like?
Maybe I don't need the robin
to make my very own robin.
I already have the robin's eye
and surely I know the rest
of the robin, surely I know
how to make a robin. Maybe
I'll make something else instead.

Stray Leaf

Nature captured the imagination
of Rupert, a singular poet, who
knew of nothing more beautiful
than the selfsame sonnet he had
written in admiration of a stray leaf
he had once found stoically hugging
the sole of his shoe as if it were
the Raft of the Medusa made flesh.

Now, on a summer's morning,
Rupert can be heard singing
the selfsame sonnet to his tea
and buttered toast as if he were
singing to a lovely young maiden
in distress on a sea of false promises.
"What comforting words dance
from my tongue!" he observed.

But singing the selfsame sonnet
every morning is not enough and
so Rupert decided he would write
another humble masterpiece,
perhaps even more profoundly moving
than the last, or the one before that.
Where to begin? he wondered,
then glanced down at his shoe.

Surely enough there was another
leaf very much resembling the one
that had given such pleasure in being
the inspiration for Rupert before.
But this leaf was different somehow,
it was a different colour for certain,
but it was also a different shape
and this caused our poet to pause.

Nothing anything like the first sonnet
came flowing along on the current
of Rupert's estuarial imagination,
nothing at all consistent with the poet
he'd been devoted to when life had been
so simple, and words not quite so complex.
Rupert studied the leaf as if the face of
a stifling foe, an inadvertent adversary.

No, this leaf didn't compel him to
trot out the words like children
marching to a pied piper's tune.
This leaf didn't compel him to do
anything but look, and look he did
down into his very soul where he
had once been living before words
were known to be clinging leaves.

Mr. & Mrs. Blackett

1.

Blackett fell upon his wife
without passion.
He glanced briefly into
the tired eyes,
no longer caring for the soul
that languished there,
and thrust himself into her.
Now, remembering a younger woman,
the woman he had once desired,
he would fasten on the details –
the taut thighs,
the firm breasts,
the unlined neck.
It would last, this interminable union,
until he heard the voice
of the younger woman urging him on.
Then he would empty himself inside her.
After, he would go downstairs
and make coffee,
while she would remain in bed.
It was during this interval
that Blackett's wife felt most alone.

2.

Mrs. Blackett hadn't intended
to reach the age of 53.
In fact, she had intended not to.
Over six miserable years,
she had amassed 540 sleeping pills.
Now they distracted and enchanted her

like swirls of tiny phosphorescent fish
at the depths of her bathroom cupboard.
As the world steadily pivoted out of control,
technology and religion gone berserk,
she hadn't an image of the future.

The future, she had always assumed,
would be about her children.
Her children, she knew,
would have blossomed
with her nurturing.
They would have managed
admirably in the world,
no matter how bleak
or terrifying it might become,
and she would have carried on,
even after death, loving them.

No children,
no future,
no sanctity to her death
through which to cherish
the ultimate, all-sacrificing love.

3.

Mr. Blackett gave the appearance
of being a robust and healthy 56,
although Mrs. Blackett knew him to be
afflicted with a rare and inevitably
disfiguring disease, one reserved
exclusively for the very selfish.
She'd hoped for a short time,
that he was becoming kinder
but his persistently puerile response

to every new problem, no matter how small
or undemanding, had betrayed her optimism.

Mr. Blackett was a man without a heart
sufficiently large enough to care.
This conclusion, in its finality,
was a sad burden to bear,
but subconsciously Mrs. Blackett
had been bearing it all along.
It was impossible to imagine herself
continuing to live with her husband,
especially in his declining years.

4.

Mr. Blackett's father had been
an excellent example of a man
who had missed one very important point:
he'd allowed himself to be generous,
only to find his nose pushed in
by greedier, *worthier* men. And so
his son would be the aggressor.

Mr. Blackett lived for himself.
It was a hard-won achievement,
although his mother had helped.
She had taught him one important lesson:
never let anyone have what doesn't
rightfully belong to them,
especially if it should
rightfully belong to you.

If anyone was to reside
behind a grandiloquent facade
of self-sufficiency

it would be Mr. Blackett –
not his all too sensitive wife.

How Mrs. Blackett had continued
on with Mr. Blackett was simple:
she had indulged in the pursuits
of the material world while giving up
the revivifying force of intimacy.
Yes, the thought of sustaining him
in his declining years was
a profoundly depressing one.

5.

Darling, where have you put my shoes?
Which shoes are those?
Why, the ones I wear on the weekend,
what other shoes would I be referring to?

There Stands the Enemy

His gun the flex of
his pathetic muscle,
there stands the enemy
as the child goes down,
her face bitten with lead.

What cruelty
there is
in the glance
of the stranger
who, in the moment
he injures,
knows nothing –

has no details,
can't see anything
of value
about those
he slays,
or leaves casually
to die.

Let the flesh fall away,
one second
he thinks,
again knowing nothing.

Let my hand be
the hand of God,
the next second
he thinks.

And what
a cruel God
he is, but not
unto himself
in his
grand dimension
of ignorance.

Bring down
the walls about
the soldiers
of Babylon,
bring down
the shadows
that light their way
to oblivion.

Psychotic Poem

Come to me,
come to me
and hold me.

Come to me
and love me,
mommy.

And then I shall kill you,
and take your disgusting body,
the same body that bore me
whole but deformed,
with the head of a withered potato,
sprouting rubbery arms and legs,
and throw it down
the filthy embankment,
littered with beer and soda bottles
and discarded tyres,
and into the river.

There to rot, to dissolve
into a million little *you's*,
to poison the fish,
to evaporate, to scatter
the toxic wastes of your soul
across the sky like cancer.

Who Could Be Ruder

Who could be ruder,
than the elderly dying
with resentment,
anguish turned to spite,
as one would never
have supposed.
Tongues so bitterly coated
lash the psychic fabric
unbidden – abrogations,
oaths muttered, not
solely in extremis,
hurrying darkness
into the bedclothes.

Her Food Being Hot

Her food
being hot
she ate,
but something
occurred to her
that,
like a cloud
of dust
falling down
from
the ceiling,
suspended
her appetite.

Later,
that night,
she resumed
eating,
having
promised herself
not to think
anymore.

Diary

The boulevards of Paris
were now unwittingly
paved in gold,
the rigid streets of New York
with myriad woes
unforetold.

The Upper Room

1.

The door to the house opens,
a tall person with a powdered face
stands formidably before me.
If this is a man, he is unlike
any other man. Sullen blue leaves
lie desiccated, scattered over
the floor of the sala drenched
in shadow, clothed in the grime
that endures along the harbour.

The staircase rises isolated
to doors looming solemnly
like sentries watching over a tomb,
so many rooms preciously hidden
from the drifting debris outside
redolent with the fumes of intimacy.
I'm led on, up the steps, and wait.
Beyond one door, now opened,
a suite of rooms staggers dimly
and the heat of sound grows full,
but not with welcoming anticipation.

Left alone, I eventually hear voices,
voices not discreetly hushed
but incisive, obliquely intransigent,
as if the awakening of birdsong
were forbidden with the opening
of the lugubrious drapes allowing in
the therapeutic light of another day.
Now the powdered face passes by,
to merge with the omnipresent haze,
one moment thudding in the heart

into the next, the futility of speaking
impinging upon tongue and nerves.

2.

He sits in the shadows, the wheels
of his wheelchair edging into the light
slanting in through the open window.
A withered figure, grey as eternal dusk,
his eyes are masked in sunglasses.
These are ageless things, these plastic
glasses, and so are the lips that know
no gender but have known too many.
Is he blind, is he morose, is he someone
who ensnares with tentacles of distrust?
Dogs can be heard rummaging below
the window on the luxuriant garbage,
teetering piles of this city's rotting jewels.

I move a chair and sit before him.
The head turns, the sunglasses fixed,
eyes on the window, peering at nothing.
It would seem appropriate to whisper,
and I make an effort to remain aloof for
each precarious moment is ripe with futility.
Amusement emanating perversely from the
crooked body topped by the head of god,
the divinity's grimace is a flattened bouquet
of hours spent languishing in a sullied bed.

3.

I glimpse the dishevelled garden,
towering palms battered by molten sky,
its rococo swimming pool empty,
tiles encrusted like oyster shells.

I have the persistent impression
of a tumorous hovel grown gargantuan
in its decrepitude, irretrievably decaying,
but feeding on itself without embarrassment.
There is only fatigue and I gesture to ask
if I might make my exit, but am held fast
by the old man's infuriatingly opulent gaze.
Now how shall I excuse himself, and go
about the business of playing the virgin?
But nothing comes from my mouth,
my disquiet overarching, overreaching
its meagre limits as I imagine nothing
but torture, and my courage collapses.

4.

My money was given and the fake name
of my Salomé uttered without fanfare.
Now would the frolicking begin and
the barking of the dogs be silenced by
the singing wheels of the wheelchair
and the song I would sing unravelling?

"Sleep doesn't grow on trees,"
said the deity, eyelids drooping,
I imagined, behind the amber lenses,
but not with the evening shadows
as they should, as they would if not
for my agitation raising the alarm —
had I paid enough, what price oblivion?

Below the window, the dogs
barked on and on and on as I,
another lonely man, mechanically
returned to confront my anxiety.
But no malevolence lay between

the light cast over the floor
and the door to my inundation.

She had arrived, in all her splendour.
"We don't grow on trees," I said
to her, and knew that in her eyes
I wasn't a stranger but a messenger.
The sunglasses were lowered and we
saw the deity gazing on in wonder.

5.

She goes a few steps ahead of me
out onto the balcony and leads us
on to another door where she stops
and turns briefly, beckoning for me
to follow her up the narrow steps
to the uppermost rooms of the house.
What intrigues me in steady deliberation
is the disappearance of the other being
she had been before her movements
had quite naturally conspired to enchant.

Her silhouette arches backwards,
and in that long curve of light
I see the wide harbour beyond
the height of our darkened room.
Is she watching me, I wonder,
hoping she is and she is,
but she is watching another,
a man altogether unknown to me.

The Frog and the Flower

The frog and the flower
dwell in peace
partly because
they share the belief
that each day
they grow more alike,
and partly because
with each day,
one to the other,
they learn to say:
now you are me.

The Roses

The roses tumble from their vase
unaware of the statue's gaze.
Now, the rain tumults, catapults
the buzzing bees into the trees.
The glowing windows of remorse
are the startled eyes of the horse
lunging over hills, daffodils,
away from me into the sea.

Little Birds

Little birds
fly away
into the storm
never to return,
their memory
a distant stillness
that echoes
in the wind.

The Wind

The wind swung by me
bearing no arrows,
not hearing my thoughts,
and in that moment
I was released from
the terrors of tomorrow.

After the Fourth

The river was filled with mud,
slowly moving, viscous red mud.
Sunday and the Fourth of July
holiday had thankfully passed
without mishap or injury.
The storm that had blown in
from the north on Friday evening
had been the single great event
of this uneventful weekend.

My guests had never seen
such fury breathing through
the trees, lashings to unhinge
the apricot horizon, and closer –
monumental sheets of mist.
I'd urged them onto the porch,
Its freshly painted boards glistening
like glass chimes laid in a row.

I was again on the deck of our ship
crossing the Aegean to Andros in
another smothering storm, my friends
huddled in the deep doorway
as the wind wound its long fingers
round the rim of the roof overhanging
the porch and softly touched our faces.

My friends, husband and wife,
with their dark eyes and a love
of luxuriating in the sun by a pool,
had a little boy, a child of seven,
who existed there on the porch
in a timeless moment of confusion.
At first irritated by our interest in

the violent swaying of the trees,
he had then been hypnotized himself,
his gaze eventually turning inward.

Was he remembering, had he seen
the same power sweep the sky
from the windows of their apartment,
the turgid green river that ran through
the city's towering citadels of glass
shimmering with muted colour?

Although safe within the porch's embrace,
it was apparent the boy, his feet twitching,
wanted to leave his mother and father and
walk off into the storm's relentless turmoil.
But he retreated into the house, his resolve
subduing his confusion, his parents unaware,
hearts filled with an unfamiliar happiness.

Their brown bodies enjoying the exhilaration,
the succulence of each moment, they themselves
were like children anticipating more excitement.
The abrupt cracking of a limb, the tree nearby,
jarred the senses and the essence of awakening
quite suddenly possessed us there in our limbo.

One after the other, we strayed into the house,
down the hallway, and into the warm shadows
of the living-room with its comfortable chairs.
The boy had vanished, perhaps to the room
that had once been mine, a room for hiding.
Was I more sensitive to their child's threshold
of wonder, having no children myself, having
therefore remained a child in my obsolescence?
I too had had to recover my immaculate sense
of wonder, and it had been an arduous task

as I'd asked only for that single window
to remain mysteriously open allowing in
the fumes that fuel sweet reckless impulse.

On Sunday, as we observed the richness
of the river and its swarming detritus,
the boy asked why the river should be red
when the torrents of rain had been white.
The river was full of the blood of mankind,
the blood of his birth, but I said nothing
at first, only wondered at this unruly metaphor.
As my thoughts progressed, the wild droplets
of rain became the profuse perspiration
in which he'd been conceived upon a city bed.

I finally answered that the transparent rainwater
had carried the colour of the soil along with it
as it had rushed over the bare riverbanks
to flow downstream thickening to the dam.
The boy was perplexed by my explanation
as I was by denying the truth of my imagining,
for I had imagined the divination of his mortality
and with it had spontaneously arisen compassion
for his mother and father, who would soon lose him.

The Foaming Crease

The foaming crease
opens wider
to increase
its grip on my
small world.

Curling outward
comes the sighing
breath of yearning
for those who endure
another sleepless night.

Lost in contemplation
the spectators tumble
into the palms
of my waiting hands
wanting an answer.

But who calls out now
from the crease,
could it be that song
of despair that hides
within our silent heat?

Bathe me now
in the warm wind
of forgetting,
in the soothing oblivion
of another alien catastrophe.
Raggedly fall the leaves
through the wounded roof
scorched open and wailing
in disbelief, never to reclaim
its shape or errant dignity.

We meet without hesitation
like the marauding flames
that rule the hour,
that infuse the empty streets
with a thrilling fervour.

We are bound by nothing,
not by the consummate will
of nature, nor nature's reason,
not by the lawless harbours
that shelter aberration.

We are tyrants only
unto ourselves
as we slip deeper
into the crease,
into the baying mouth.

Now to heal our aching
thoughts like shadows
rising up before the fire
that comes unbidden to lie
with us in our fragrant beds.

Far away, the fire rages on
while here within, our lips
are left searching for the words
never to undo what's been done,
never to deny our moment.

Creperie du Pradet, St. Hippolyte du Fort, France, was destroyed by fire, purportedly arson, on the night of 22nd March 2012, the conflagration made known to the police at 1:15am.